I0409772

CHAPTER 1

STEPPING INTO THE WORLD OF ETSY

Welcome to the fascinating universe of Etsy entrepreneurship! This book is your ultimate roadmap to establishing and steering a prosperous venture on Etsy, a well-established international platform known for its collection of unique, handcrafted items.

We start our journey by unraveling the secrets of Etsy – its core idea, its progression, its operations, and reasons it's an unparalleled arena for business enthusiasts like you. Etsy stands as an extraordinary digital bazaar connecting artists, vintage collectors, craft enthusiasts, and customers from every corner of the world. Its unique identity stems from its focus on handcrafted, vintage, and crafting supplies, fostering an environment that emphasizes personal relationships between the buyer and the seller.

Etsy was conceived with the aim to revolutionize commerce, contributing towards a more sustainable world, by bridging the gap between independent creators and consumers in search of one-of-a-kind items.

At its core, Etsy seeks to instill a human touch in e-commerce by facilitating direct transactions between consumers and creators. This approach not only kindles creativity but also acts as a support system to independent businesses.

On Etsy, the act of selling extends beyond listing products. It's about narrating a story, sharing your creative journey, the inspiration behind your work, and the intricate craftwork that goes into each piece. This intimate touch cultivates a culture of admiration for handmade goods, nurturing a profound sense of community. For those driven by the urge to create unique items, Etsy offers an unrivaled platform to transform your craft into a successful venture. Etsy puts a spotlight on individuality and craftsmanship, allowing creativity to flourish and distinct products to connect with their ideal customers.

When Etsy sprouted in 2005, it was rooted in a potent yet straightforward vision: to keep commerce human. Recognizing the impact of e-commerce on retail, Etsy's founders identified a need for a platform to enable artisans and creators to sell their unique, handcrafted, and vintage goods, thus embracing creativity and personal connection.

Over the years, Etsy has steadfastly held onto its founding vision, continually providing a platform for small-scale businesses and individual artisans to prosper, fostering an environment that promotes creativity, originality, and individual expression.

Etsy's dedication to sustainability further reinforces its vision, striving to be a marketplace that respects and preserves the environment. In 2020, Etsy became the first global e-commerce company to offset 100% of carbon emissions from shipping, reiterating its commitment to a sustainable, human-centric approach to commerce.

Since its inception in 2005, Etsy has evolved from a small site selling only wooden items to an extensive global marketplace. Despite some hiccups along the way, Etsy has remained loyal to its mission: to empower individuals to reshape the workings of the global economy. Etsy's evolution represents a balance of upholding its core vision while adapting to the dynamic landscape of e-commerce.

Etsy's operating model is straightforward yet effective. Anyone can open a shop on Etsy free of charge, list their products for a small fee, and reach a global audience. What sets Etsy apart is its commitment to unique, handcrafted, and vintage items.

Navigating Etsy isn't simply shopping; it's a journey through a global bazaar of individual shops, each with its unique tale.

Deciding to initiate an online business involves selecting the right platform. With its emphasis on handmade and vintage items, Etsy presents a unique opportunity for artisans, crafters, and collectors. Achieving success on Etsy is often marked by creating unique products, forging connections with customers, and maintaining a professional online shop. Successful Etsy entrepreneurs typically share common traits: a deep passion for their craft, excellent customer service, professionalism, adaptability, and persistence.

There's an abundance of success stories from people who started small on Etsy and built profitable businesses. These stories serve as an inspiration for prospective Etsy entrepreneurs. The thought of initiating an online venture can stir up a mix of emotions – exhilaration and intimidation. However, as seen throughout this chapter, Etsy's distinctive platform offers an empowering and supportive environment for crafters, artisans, and vintage collectors to launch and grow their businesses.

Success on Etsy is achievable but requires effort, patience, and a passion for your craft.

With the right dedication and approach, you can turn your passion into a prosperous online business.

As we conclude this chapter, you'll not only possess a deeper understanding of Etsy, but will also feel motivated by the successful trajectories of individuals who carved their path in this marketplace.

CHAPTER 2

UNVEILING YOUR CREATIVE SANCTUARY

Embarking on the exhilarating journey of creating your own Etsy shop requires a careful and deliberate approach. It's more than just setting up an online store; it's an artistic sanctuary where your creations will come to life, connecting with admirers and patrons from every corner of the world. As you step into this realm of creativity, let's explore the essential steps to craft your Etsy masterpiece.

Planning Your Shop's Essence:

Before diving into the depths of your creative sanctuary, take a moment to envision what you wish to showcase to the world. Define your unique selling proposition, understand your target audience, and consider how you want your brand to be perceived. Your shop's name, logo, product listings, and shop story all contribute to your overall identity. Strive for consistency, authenticity, and appeal, reflecting the true nature of your artistic venture.

Choosing a Captivating Shop Name:

Your shop's name is the calling card of your brand, so it's essential to choose one that captures the essence of your creations.

Let your products speak through the name; it should give potential customers a glimpse of what you offer. Stand out from the crowd with a memorable and easily pronounceable name that reflects your uniqueness.

Setting Shop Preferences:

Customize your shop preferences to ensure smooth operations. Select your preferred language, country, and currency to create a seamless experience for your global audience. Let the rhythm of your shop's activities align with the time zone that fits your production and shipping needs.

Crafting an Irresistible Product Range:

Your product selection is the heart and soul of your Etsy shop. Embrace your passion and skills to curate a collection that resonates with your artistry. Research market demand and explore niche markets to find the sweet spot that sets you apart while appealing to your target customers. Consider pricing, logistics, and sustainability as you shape your creative offerings.

Designing an Alluring Shop Banner and Logo:

Visual appeal plays a crucial role in attracting customers to your shop. Create an eye-catching shop banner that showcases your products, promotions, or your shop's essence. Your logo should be simple yet memorable, representing your shop's focus and aligning with your brand identity.

Weaving Your Artistic Narrative:

Tell the captivating tale of your artistic journey through your shop's story. Share your inspiration, the process behind your creations, and the factors that make your shop unique. Engage your potential customers on a personal level and create a sense of connection through your heartfelt narrative.

Establishing Clear Shop Policies:

Building trust with your customers is vital in the artisanal realm of Etsy. Define your shop policies with clarity and fairness, covering payment methods, shipping details, returns, and exchanges. By setting clear expectations, you ensure a positive shopping experience for your customers.

Unleashing Your Creative Odyssey:

Your Etsy shop is more than an online store; it's a reflection of your passion, creativity, and authenticity.

As you embark on this creative odyssey, let your unique voice shine through every aspect of your shop.

Embrace the individuality that Etsy thrives on and let your artistry captivate the world. With the foundation laid, you are now ready to unleash your Etsy masterpiece and embark on a journey that celebrates the boundless creativity within you.

CHAPTER 3

CRAFTING ENCHANTING PRODUCT LISTINGS

Welcome to the realm of Etsy magic, where your artistry meets entrepreneurship to create an unforgettable shopping experience. In this chapter, we'll explore the secrets to transform your virtual storefront into an enchanting showcase that captivates potential customers, showcases your unique creations, and drives sales. Let's delve into the details and learn how to craft product listings that truly shine on Etsy.

Captivating Visual Stories:

Embrace the art of visual storytelling through your product photography. Let each image weave a spell of enchantment, capturing the essence of your creations with natural light and a clean, uncluttered backdrop. Zoom in to reveal the intricate details and unique features that set your items apart. Showcase variations and customizations, letting customers envision the possibilities. Take them on a journey with lifestyle shots, showing how your art can enrich their lives. Captivating photography will be the key to capturing hearts and sparking interest in your creations.

Magical Descriptions:

Unveil the enchantment of your products through captivating descriptions. Speak directly to your ideal customers, understanding their desires and needs. Go beyond listing features; paint a vivid picture of how your art can transform their world. Embrace the power of storytelling, sharing the inspiration and passion behind each creation. Use descriptive language to create an emotional connection, allowing customers to feel the magic within your products. Provide all the necessary details to empower them to make informed choices.

Harmony in Pricing:

The art of pricing lies in finding the perfect balance between value and cost. Consider the resources invested in crafting each item and research the market to set competitive prices. Let the magic of perceived value justify the worth of your unique creations. Offer different pricing tiers to cater to a diverse audience. Use promotions and limited-time offers to entice customers into your artistic realm. Be adaptable and adjust prices as needed, maintaining harmony with market trends.

Spells of Discovery:

Unlock the realm of keywords to enchant seekers with your offerings. Select tags that resonate with your ideal customers, guiding them to your art. Embrace specificity, utilizing long-tail keywords to connect with niche markets. Maximize your opportunities with multiple tags to widen your reach. Stay attuned to market trends and adjust your keywords to cast spells of discovery on potential customers.

Customization and Choice:

Empower customers to co-create their dreams by offering variations and customizations. Embrace the allure of choice, whether in colors, sizes, or materials. Showcase images that unveil the magic of each option, inviting patrons to find their perfect match. Provide transparency in pricing and production time to build trust in your offerings. Let the realm of customization be a gateway to forging lasting connections with customers.

The Power of Social Proof:

In the realm of customer reviews and social proof, trust blossoms like flowers in bloom. Nurture exceptional customer service to sow the seeds of satisfaction. Follow up with personalized messages, thanking customers for their patronage and encouraging reviews. Let the packaging carry gentle requests for feedback, making it effortless for customers to share their thoughts. Display a tapestry of praise on your shop's main page, letting the magic of social proof deepen the allure of your art.

Chapter Conclusion: Your Enchanted Journey

As we conclude this chapter, embrace the artistry of crafting enchanting product listings. Each element weaves together to create a symphony of enchantment, drawing customers into your artistic realm. Continuously refine your craft, attuning your artistry to the ever-changing rhythm of the market. With this knowledge, you are now poised to cast a spell of allure and captivate the hearts of seekers as they discover the magic of your creations. As we embark on the next chapter, prepare to unravel the secrets of effective marketing strategies, further unveiling the power of your Etsy odyssey. Embrace your art, trust your instincts, and let your creativity soar like a symphony of stars in the boundless skies of Etsy.

CHAPTER 4

UNLEASHING THE ART OF ENCHANTING MARKETING

Welcome to a realm where marketing magic weaves its spell over your Etsy shop. In this chapter, we'll embark on an extraordinary journey to explore effective marketing strategies that will amplify your shop's reach and captivate your target audience. So, brace yourself for an enchanting adventure as we dive into the world of Etsy enchantment.

The Enchanting Identity:

Your shop's identity is the heart of its charm. Craft a compelling personality that resonates with your ideal customers. Define your shop's aura, whether it's whimsical, elegant, or eco-friendly. Create a memorable shop name and logo that symbolizes your brand's essence. Embrace consistent visuals with captivating colors, typography, and imagery. Craft a mesmerizing brand story that sparks wonder and forges an emotional connection with your audience.

The Magic of Social Media:

Unleash the power of social media to connect with your target audience. Choose the right platforms where your ideal customers gather. Enchant your followers with engaging content that showcases your products' magic. Embrace user-generated content and encourage interaction. Collaborate with influencers and bloggers to extend your reach and captivate new audiences.

The Enchantment of SEO:

Unravel the secrets of Search Engine Optimization to illuminate your shop in search results. Delve into the alchemy of keyword research to discover the spells that attract seekers. Infuse strategic keywords into your shop's title and about section.

Enchant your product titles and descriptions with captivating keywords. Use tags to weave a spell of discoverability.

Engaging with Enchantment:

Engage with your audience to nurture lasting relationships. Respond to inquiries with personalized attention. Foster a sense of community by encouraging user-generated content. Organize enchanting contests and giveaways to captivate your audience. Embrace the art of feedback and reviews to build trust.

The Enchanted Emails:

Harness the power of email marketing to stay woven into your audience's hearts. Create an enchanting email list with exclusive offers. Segment your list to personalize your messages. Craft mesmerizing email content that unveils new products and conjures captivating stories. Use automation to send timely reminders and offers.

Chapter Conclusion: Embrace the Enchantment

As we conclude this chapter of enchanting marketing strategies, you hold the key to unlock your Etsy shop's true potential. Your magical brand identity, social media enchantments, SEO spells, and engaging interactions create a symphony of enchantment that draws customers into your captivating realm. Remember, marketing is an ongoing journey of experimentation and adaptation. Continuously explore new enchantments, analyze your results, and adapt your strategies to create the most captivating spells.

CHAPTER 5

THE PATH OF CUSTOMER ENCHANTMENT

Step into the realm of customer enchantment, where every interaction holds the promise of magic and delight. In this chapter, we'll unlock the secrets of exceptional customer service, uncovering strategies that will transform your Etsy shop into an enchanted haven for shoppers. By weaving together empathy, personalized experiences, and proactive solutions, you can create a loyal customer base and leave an indelible mark in the hearts of those who cross your path. So, let's set forth on this enchanting journey and explore the art of customer enchantment.

The Art of Enchanting Experiences:

Exceptional customer service is not just a goal; it's an enchanting journey that begins with every customer. We'll explore how to go beyond mere satisfaction and create magical experiences for each shopper. By setting high standards, embracing proactive solutions, and building customer trust, you'll forge lasting connections and cultivate a loyal following for your Etsy shop.

Embracing the Power of Empathy:

In the land of customer enchantment, empathy reigns supreme. Discover the transformative power of understanding and relating to your customers' needs. Be responsive and attentive, listening with your heart to their desires and concerns. Personalize your interactions to make every customer feel cherished and valued. Show that you care deeply about their journey with your shop.

Turning Challenges into Enchanted Solutions:

On the enchanted path, challenges are opportunities in disguise. Learn to embrace them with grace and turn them into moments of enchantment. Apologize sincerely for any inconvenience and take swift action to resolve issues. Communicate transparently about your plans to restore harmony. Show customers that they are at the heart of your quest for solutions.

Enchanting Surprises and Beyond:

Step into the realm of enchantment by sprinkling surprises along the way. Personalize each customer's journey with unexpected delights, like handcrafted notes of appreciation or a small magical gift. Anticipate their needs and exceed their expectations, making them feel like they've stumbled upon a treasure trove of wonders.

The Magic of Glowing Reviews:

In the realm of customer enchantment, glowing reviews are the essence of magic. Learn to cultivate these enchanting testimonials from your customers. Ask for reviews graciously and provide simple ways for customers to share their experiences. Respond with gratitude and warmth to each review, kindling a sense of kinship with your buyers. Share their enchanting words across your social realms.

Harnessing the Wisdom of Customer Feedback:

In the enchanted forest of your Etsy shop, customer feedback is a valuable compass. Embrace it as a guiding light to improve and grow. Seek feedback proactively through post-purchase messages or thoughtfully crafted surveys. Listen with humility and an open mind to uncover hidden insights. Transform feedback into magical improvements that surprise and enchant your customers.

CHAPTER 6

THE POWER OF EXPANSION

Step into the realm of boundless possibilities, where your Etsy business takes flight on the wings of expansion. In this chapter, we embark on an exhilarating journey to unlock the secrets of effective scaling and growth. Scaling is more than a destination; it's a transformational adventure that requires innovation, adaptability, and a relentless pursuit of excellence. Let's set sail on this voyage of discovery, uncovering novel strategies that will elevate your Etsy shop to unprecedented heights of prosperity.

The Symphony of Streamlined Efficiency

Efficiency is the symphony that sets the tone for your scaling journey. Fine-tune your processes, eliminate bottlenecks, and orchestrate seamless workflows. By automating repetitive tasks, crafting foolproof standard operating procedures, and embracing cutting-edge software solutions, you'll conduct the grandest of performances, where efficiency takes center stage.

Navigating the Treasures of Inventory Mastery

Unlock the hidden treasures of inventory mastery on your scaling expedition. Embrace the art of demand forecasting, optimize stock levels, and navigate the labyrinth of supply chain management. By practicing just-in-time inventory techniques and fostering strong supplier partnerships, you'll chart a course that leads to smooth sailing even amidst turbulent seas.

Venturing Beyond the Horizon of Opportunity

Beyond the horizon lies a world of untapped opportunities awaiting your discovery. Venture into new markets, diversify your product offerings, and forge powerful alliances with like-minded creators. Envision wholesale possibilities, explore uncharted sales channels, and dare to embrace the unexplored territories of growth.

Navigating the Labyrinth of Operational Mastery

In the labyrinth of scaling, operational mastery is the key to your success. Navigate skillfully through the intricacies of workflows, wield the power of project management tools, and embrace the magic of e-commerce innovations. With a keen eye for analytics and continuous improvement, you'll chart a course towards operational excellence.

The Kaleidoscope of Diverse Creations

Within the kaleidoscope of scaling, a spectrum of diverse creations awaits. Expand your product line, introducing enchanting variations and personalized touches that resonate with your customers. Unlock the art of testing new ideas, and collaborate with fellow artisans to create limited-edition wonders that captivate hearts and minds.

Assembling the Dream Team of Visionaries

In the pursuit of scaling greatness, assemble a dream team of visionary minds. Identify the talents and skills needed to fuel your business growth. Seek out passionate individuals who share your vision and breathe life into your aspirations.

Cultivate a culture of collaboration and empowerment that propels your team towards remarkable achievements.

Embracing Growth as a Perpetual Odyssey

As we conclude this chapter, remember that scaling is an odyssey, a perpetual journey of evolution. Embrace a growth mindset, ever-curious and open to new horizons. Tune in to the melodies of market trends, the whispers of customer desires, and the winds of technological change. Let your customer-centric spirit steer your course as you continue on the path of perpetual expansion.

Chapter Conclusion: Ascending to New Heights

In this chapter of boundless expansion, you have ascended to new heights. By unleashing the power of streamlined efficiency, mastering inventory, venturing into new realms of opportunity, optimizing operations, diversifying your creations, and building a team of visionaries, you have harnessed the winds of growth. With every step, you have set sail towards a prosperous future.

The next chapter awaits, where we will embark on a voyage of marketing mastery. From crafting mesmerizing brand stories to conjuring the magic of social media, influencer collaborations, and targeted advertising, we will unravel the secrets of captivating your audience. So, brace yourself for this exhilarating journey as we chart a course into the enchanting world of marketing marvels.

CHAPTER 7

ILLUMINATING PATHWAYS TO ETSY TRIUMPH

Welcome to the realm of Etsy triumph, where effective marketing holds the key to your success. As we delve into this chapter, we embark on an expedition of discovery, uncovering unique marketing strategies tailored specifically for Etsy sellers. Marketing is not just about promotion; it's about forging connections, showcasing your shop's distinct value, and kindling the flames of growth. So, let's ignite the spark of creativity and explore the strategies that will propel your Etsy business towards unrivaled success.

Crafting a Radiant Brand Identity

Amidst the vibrant Etsy marketplace, a strong brand identity becomes your guiding light. Define your brand personality, let it shine through your communications, and weave captivating brand stories. By designing a memorable logo, curating a consistent visual identity, and creating a seamless brand experience, you'll cast a radiant glow that draws customers to your shop like moths to a flame.

Igniting Social Media Magic

In the digital realm, the magic of social media awaits your command.

Harness its power to expand your reach, kindle brand awareness, and ignite customer engagement. Sail through platforms like Instagram, Facebook, Pinterest, or TikTok, crafting a content strategy that resonates with your audience and sparks conversations that spread like wildfire.

Illuminating the Path of SEO Brilliance

In the labyrinth of the online world, SEO becomes your guiding beacon. Illuminate your Etsy shop with well-researched keywords, optimized product titles, and compelling descriptions. Navigate through the realm of tags and wield the art of image optimization to ensure your shop is discovered by eager explorers seeking your creations.

Collaborating with Luminaries of Influence

Befriend the luminaries of influence, the stars who shine brightly in the sky of social media. Partner with influencers and bloggers who share your passions and values, and let their light shine upon your products. Through their recommendations and endorsements, you'll create a celestial trail that leads customers straight to your Etsy galaxy.

Engaging Hearts and Minds

In the heart of the Etsy cosmos, engagement is the key to forging lasting connections. Respond promptly to inquiries, encourage user-generated content, and host captivating contests and giveaways. Illuminate your audience with valuable content, from tutorials to live Q&A sessions, and bask in the warmth of their loyalty.

Unleashing the Power of Stellar Email Marketing

Like constellations in the night sky, email marketing guides your customers on a journey of loyalty. Build a constellation of subscribers by offering incentives, then craft celestial content that resonates with their desires. Automate your communications to ensure consistent brilliance, and track the stars of analytics to refine your approach.

Chapter Conclusion: Embracing the Brilliance of Etsy Triumph

As we conclude this chapter of illumination, remember that marketing is the celestial light that guides your Etsy journey. By building a radiant brand identity, igniting social media magic, mastering the art of SEO brilliance, collaborating with luminaries of influence, engaging hearts and minds, and unleashing the power of stellar email marketing, you shine a light that draws customers near.

CHAPTER 8

CUSTOMER CARE AND LOYALTY FOR ETSY PROSPERITY

Welcome to the realm of customer care and loyalty, where every step along the enchanted path can lead to Etsy prosperity. In this chapter, we will embark on a journey to discover the significance of exceptional customer service and tailored retention strategies for Etsy sellers. By understanding the unique journey of your customers, offering responsive and personalized support, crafting unforgettable experiences, implementing effective customer retention initiatives, utilizing valuable feedback, and forging lasting relationships, you will lay the foundation for sustained success in the enchanting world of Etsy. So let's embark on this magical expedition to unravel the secrets of customer care and loyalty and how they can lead your Etsy business to prosperity.

Unveiling the Customer's Enchanted Journey

To provide exceptional customer service, it is essential to unveil the enchanted journey of your customers. From the very moment they discover your Etsy shop to their delightful post-purchase experience, every touchpoint should be a magical encounter.

By understanding their needs, preferences, and concerns, you can tailor your offerings to exceed their expectations at every step of their journey.

Weaving the Threads of Responsive Support

Responsive support is the enchanted thread that weaves a strong connection between you and your customers. Timely responses and helpful assistance can work wonders in creating a positive and enchanting experience. By promptly addressing inquiries and concerns with empathy and efficiency, you can build trust and loyalty among your customers.

Enchanting Personalization for Lasting Impressions

The art of personalization is a magical key to creating lasting impressions. Tailoring your interactions and offerings to each customer's preferences and interests can make them feel truly special. By collecting customer data and using it to curate personalized experiences, you'll enchant your customers and make them feel valued.

Casting Spells of Customer Retention

Customer retention holds the secret spell to Etsy prosperity. Enchant your customers with loyalty programs that bestow rewards and exclusive benefits. Create VIP experiences for your most devoted patrons and keep them enchanted with engaging email marketing campaigns. Encourage them to spread the magic by casting the spell of referral programs.

Gaining Wisdom from Customer Feedback

The wisdom of customer feedback is like a magical elixir for growth. Embrace the enchantment of surveys and feedback forms to gather valuable insights. Listen to their enchanting product reviews and engage with them on social media platforms. Direct communication can reveal the most potent spells for your Etsy success.

Forging Lasting Bonds with Customers

In the mystical realm of Etsy, forging lasting bonds with customers is the true treasure. Consistently providing exceptional service, staying connected through personalized outreach, and offering special rewards can cultivate loyalty.

Create an enchanted community where customers can interact and support each other, and personalize your interactions to create memorable connections.

Chapter Conclusion: Embracing the Magic of Etsy Prosperity

As we conclude this enchanted chapter, remember that customer care and loyalty are the magic spells that can lead your Etsy business to prosperity. By unveiling the customer's journey, providing responsive support, personalizing experiences, casting retention spells, embracing customer feedback, and forging lasting bonds, you'll create a realm of devoted customers who will be your greatest advocates. Let the enchantment of your Etsy business spread far and wide, drawing in new admirers and propelling your prosperity to new heights.

CHAPTER 9

THE WINGS OF GROWTH

Welcome to a realm of boundless possibilities, where the wings of growth carry your Etsy business to new heights. This chapter is a voyage of discovery, where we will unravel the secrets of scaling your Etsy empire with finesse and flair.

Discover the alchemy of operational brilliance as we fine-tune every aspect of your Etsy venture. Unravel the secrets to streamline workflows, eliminating every obstacle that hinders your flight. Embrace automation to liberate time and energy, empowering you to focus on your creative magic. Weave enchantment into your inventory management, ensuring your creations are always ready to take flight into the hearts of eager customers. Let the symphony of efficiency conduct a harmonious dance, enchanting your team and patrons alike.

Compose a symphony of captivating products, each note a melody that resonates with your customers' souls. Embark on a journey of market research, discovering the desires that lay dormant, awaiting your artistic touch. Expand your repertoire with innovative variations and complementary additions, weaving a tale of versatility and allure. Venture into new product categories, exploring uncharted realms, and weaving an enchanting tapestry that captivates the hearts of your audience.

Prepare to venture into uncharted territories, where new sales channels await your artistry. Soar into the skies of e-commerce platforms, where new audiences eagerly anticipate your creations. Cast your spells on social media platforms, mesmerizing with visual storytelling that leaves a lasting impression.

Forge alliances with fellow artisans and retailers, joining forces to weave an even grander enchantment. Step into the spotlight of craft fairs and trade shows, where face-to-face encounters spark connections that transcend the virtual realm.

As your Etsy empire takes flight, unite a stellar team that shares your vision and passion. Carve out the roles that form the heart of your operation, seeking artisans who breathe life into your dreams. Handpick the devoted souls who will join you on this soaring adventure. Delegate responsibilities with trust and empower your team to unleash their creativity. Foster a culture of collaboration and growth, where each member flourishes like a star in the night sky.

Enchant the world with the spell of branding and marketing, weaving a tapestry that captures hearts far and wide. Define your brand's essence, a story that ignites the imagination of your audience. Set your sights on the target market, crafting messages that resonate with their deepest desires. Imbue every touchpoint with your brand's magic, from your Etsy shop to social media realms. Harness the power of digital spells, engaging in content marketing, influencer partnerships, and captivating visuals that echo in the minds of your patrons.

Master the enigma of financial wizardry, ensuring your Etsy empire flourishes with abundance. Chart your course with a comprehensive financial plan, forecasting the winds of prosperity. Unveil the secrets of profit margins and pricing strategy, ensuring each creation takes flight with the promise of success. Seek out the resources needed to fuel your growth, exploring investment and financing options with wisdom. Control your inventory and expenses like a seasoned navigator, ensuring your journey is steady and secure. Analyze the flight patterns of your financial metrics, guiding your Etsy empire with informed decisions.

Embrace the flight of triumph that lies ahead.
Your Etsy empire is destined for new heights, soaring beyond horizons that once seemed out of reach.
Be steadfast in your quest for growth, adapting to the winds of change with

grace and courage.

CHAPTER 10

UNVEILING THE SECRETS OF ETSY ENCHANTMENT

Welcome to a realm of boundless possibilities, where the secrets of sustained success in the magical world of Etsy await your discovery. In this chapter, we shall embark on an extraordinary journey, traversing the enchanted landscape of continuous improvement, captivating customer loyalty, and staying ahead in a realm teeming with creative brilliance. Prepare to unlock the hidden powers that will propel your Etsy business to new heights of prosperity and enchantment.

As we set forth, we must heed the call of customer retention and loyalty —a force that binds the threads of triumph together. Behold the art of exceptional customer service, a spell that weaves a tapestry of delight with every interaction. Engage your customers in a dance of personalized experiences, where their dreams are met with bespoke offerings. Foster a sense of belonging with a customer loyalty program, a bewitching enchantment that rewards their loyalty and devotion. Let the winds of social media carry whispers of your brand, uniting a community of loyal followers who sing your praises.

In the heart of the journey lies the realm of product quality and innovation —the alchemy that transmutes ordinary creations into extraordinary works of art. Listen to the whispers of customer feedback, for it holds the key to perfecting your craft. Embrace sustainability as a guiding principle, endearing eco-conscious souls to your magical creations. Explore the uncharted territories of design and creativity, for therein lies the spark of eternal fascination. Stay attuned to the cosmic dance of market trends, a celestial navigation that keeps your magic one step ahead of the rest.

In the depths of the quest, we shall confront the challenges of staying ahead in a competitive marketplace—a realm where uniqueness is the elixir of triumph. Peer through the veils of your competitors, discerning their offerings and forging your own path of distinctiveness. Let your Unique Selling Proposition (USP) be the guiding star that sets your brand ablaze with brilliance. Illuminate the firmament with exceptional customer service, kindling the devotion of every soul who crosses your path.

In the shadows, we find the realm of nurturing your online reputation—a sphere where the echoes of trust and credibility resonate in the digital ether. Listen to the whispers of online conversations, responding with grace to both praise and critique. Let customer testimonials weave a web of enchantment, captivating new seekers with tales of wondrous experiences. Tend to the garden of your online reputation, a sanctuary of authenticity and appreciation.

Amidst the trials, we encounter the realm of embracing feedback for continuous improvement—a realm where every suggestion is a stepping stone to greater enchantment. Seek the wisdom of your patrons, for they hold the keys to unlocking the hidden mysteries of your craft. Respond with gratitude to their offerings of wisdom, for they hold the map to unexplored territories of enchantment. Embrace the spirit of evolution, forever metamorphosing like a radiant butterfly that emerges from the chrysalis.

In the twilight, we discover the realm of adapting to changing customer needs and market trends—a world where adaptability is the compass that guides you through shifting currents. Observe the dance of customer behavior, attuning yourself to the rhythm of their desires. Embrace the art of agility, adjusting your course to navigate the ever-changing winds of market trends.

Embody sustainability and social responsibility, for they resonate with the hearts of modern seekers.

Embrace the secrets of Etsy enchantment, for they shall lead you to eternal prosperity.

Let your Etsy business become a beacon of inspiration, a haven of enchantment, and a realm of everlasting prosperity.

www.ingramcontent.com/pod-product-compliance
Lightning Source LLC
Chambersburg PA
CBHW082231290526
45794CB00009B/3754